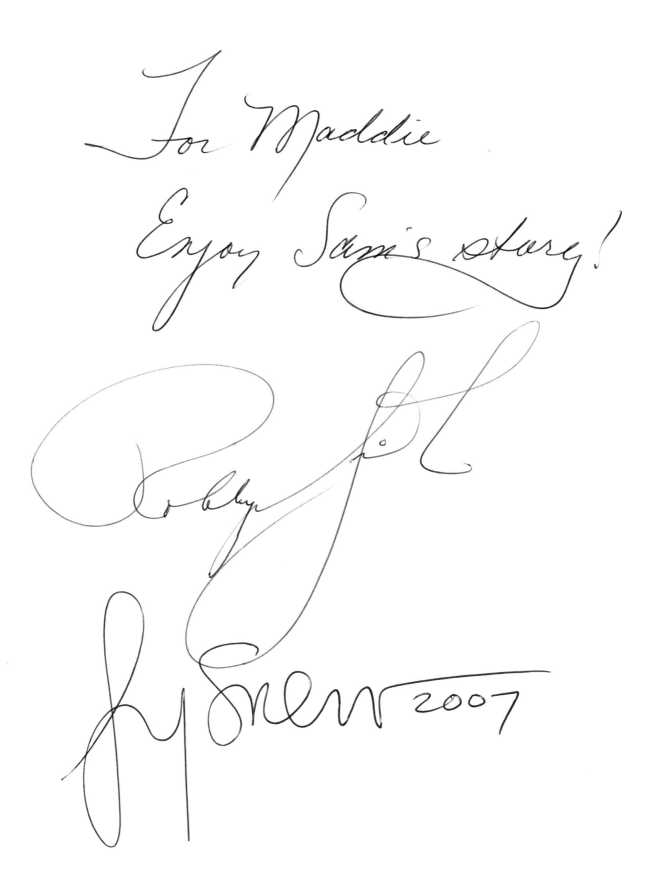

For Maddie
Enjoy Sam's story!

Robyn

Ly Brew 2007

Saving Samantha

A True Story

By Robbyn Smith van Frankenhuyzen

Illustrated by Gijsbert van Frankenhuyzen

This book is dedicated to the memory of our parents;
Bep and André van Frankenhuyzen and Trudy and Richard Smith,
who encouraged our interest in nature.

And also to our wonderful friend and mentor, Russell McKee.
Thank you for your continued support and encouragement.

Robbyn and Gijsbert

Many thanks to Louise Sagaert and her staff at Wildside Rehabilitation
Center for all you do for the injured and orphaned; Kenneth DeWeerd D.V.M. for
sharing his compassion and skill for injured animals with me. Thanks to Carl Sams
and Jean Stoick for sharing your resources with us and to John Arnsman for
answering all those fox trivia questions I asked.

Sleeping Bear Press
310 North Main Street, Suite 300
Chelsea, MI 48118
www.sleepingbearpress.com

THOMSON
GALE

Sleeping Bear Press

Sleeping Bear Press is an imprint of The Gale Group, Inc.,
a business of The Thomson Corporation.

Printed and bound in Canada.

10 9 8 7 6 5 4 3 2 1

Library of Congress Cataloging-in-Publication Data

Frankenhuyzen, Robbyn Smith van.
Saving Samantha: a true story / written by Robbyn Smith van Frankenhuyzen ;
illustrated by Gijsbert van Frankenhuyzen.
p. cm.
ISBN 1-58536-220-4
1. Red fox—Anecdotes—Juvenile literature. 2. Wildlife rescue—Juvenile literature.
3. Wildlife reintroduction—Juvenile literature. [1. Red fox. 2. Foxes. 3. Wildlife rescue.
4. Wildlife reintroduction. 5. Diaries.] I. Frankenhuyzen, Gijsbert van. II. Title.
QL737.C22F72 2003
599.775—dc22   2003025871

INTRODUCTION

Just like the message in our first book, *Adopted by an Owl*, our ultimate goal in caring for injured wildlife is to rehabilitate and release them back into the wild. We do this under strict state and federal regulations.

Nature journaling is an enjoyable part of our daily lives on Hazel Ridge Farm. Our 40-acre farm has five miles of trails that weave through wetlands, woodlots, and open fields. Daily walks lead to many discoveries, and recording them with words and sketches comes as naturally as breathing.

The relaxed writing style of journaling sets no rules and expects no masterpiece. In journals we can write or draw whatever we want, whenever and however it suits us.

We do it because it is fun. We do it because our memories are not as reliable as they once were. But mostly we do it as a legacy for our daughters Kelly and Heather, so they will remember not only the big events, but also the small natural wonders that fill their lives as they grow up on the farm.

Saving Samantha could never have been written without our journals. The journal entries in this book are actual observations of Samantha's return to the wild. Enjoy.

—Robbyn and Gijsbert van Frankenhuyzen

ABOUT THE AUTHOR AND ILLUSTRATOR

This is the second book Robbyn and Gijsbert have worked on together about wildlife rehabilitation. The first, *Adopted by an Owl*, was published in 2001. Since 1980 they have lived on their 40-acre farm in Bath, Michigan, with their daughters Heather and Kelly. The family has raised and released many injured and orphaned animals over the years, documenting each special story in their journals. Their family farm can be visited online at http://my.voyager.net/-robbyn/

One sunny spring morning, after all the farm animals had been tended to, Robbyn and the family dog, Myles, set off for their morning walk. Robbyn was eager to check out the young fox family living in the den at the farthest corner of their 40-acre farm.

The meadows were bursting with a wild display of springtime color. Tweets, twitters, and trills filled the air. From the call of the regal sandhill crane to the solemn *jug-o-rum* of the bullfrog, each creature shared its song.

Up and over the hill, Myles froze...his ears alert to a distant sound. Within seconds, Robbyn recognized the high-pitched yelps of an animal in distress and knew it was coming from the fox den.

Just outside the den, a young fox pup was struggling to free its leg from a rusty trap. The leg was twisted at an odd angle and, since fur-trapping season wouldn't start until November, Robbyn knew someone had intentionally set out to capture a pup.

"It's okay, little fox, it's okay," she whispered. Her soothing voice and gentle touch calmed the wary pup as she pried open the trap. With the frightened fox safely nestled in her jacket, Robbyn and Myles raced home

With help from her family, Robbyn was able to align the broken leg bones and wrap a wet plaster cast around the pup's leg. Samantha, as the family came to call the young vixen, spent her first week healing in a small cage in the kitchen.

May 4th
I've decided to start a "fox journal" to keep track of our
young friend. Samantha looks pretty pitiful and quite
unhappy about the clumsy cast. She clunks around her
small cage searching for a way to escape. Myles sleeps
next to the cage and that seems to comfort the pup.

In the beginning the timid fox was wary of her strange new family, but it wasn't long before her curiosity won over her fears. Her favorite napping spots were cuddled up next to Myles or curled contentedly on Robbyn's lap.

May 14th
*Sam's getting around pretty well now, so I've decided to block
off the kitchen and leave her cage door open, giving her free
run of the kitchen. She pokes her nose in every corner, finding
dust balls and other treasures. Myles follows patiently, like
a mother protecting her child.*

May 16th
At mealtime, Myles and Sam share the same bowls.

After weeks of living in the safety of the house it was time to introduce Samantha to the outdoors. Farm chores became quite an adventure for Samantha as she hobbled beside Robbyn every morning.

June 14th
Sam didn't know what to make of Black, our Tennessee Walker. She inched closer to get a better sniff of this giant beast, but a loud, wet snort from Black's nose drove her safely between my feet.

June 20th
Well, I knew it had to happen sometime. Samantha had a run-in with
Igor, the tough old rooster who has been the barnyard bully for years. Igor
chased poor Samantha around the pasture until she finally scrambled
safely under the tractor. She stayed there until Myles coaxed her out.

Spring passed and summer settled in. Robbyn removed the cast, pleased with her handiwork. Sam's leg had healed just like new. When it was time to vaccinate the dogs and cats on the farm, Sam was included. She was truly a member of the family.

June 30th
Sam hunts monarchs and grasshoppers in and around the cosmos while I weed the carrot patch. Her tireless leaping and pouncing may seem like play, but she is learning valuable hunting skills.

July 7th
A clown act unfolds as Samantha tugs and pulls at the rickety scarecrow. They are performing like dance partners, dipping and swaying in front of a row of young cabbage heads. Corvis, the family crow, annoyed at the intruder, heckled her from a safe distance.

Samantha now had her own roomy cage outside that she could run and dig and play in. During the day she could come and go as she pleased, but Robbyn always locked her up at night to keep her out of trouble. Samantha's favorite games were "harass the cats" and "chase the chickens," but she always steered clear of Igor.

July 14th
It tickles me to watch Myles and Sam race through the pasture,
zigzagging through a maze of horses and sheep. They leap and
pounce on anything that moves. Samantha's greatest pleasure
seems to be catching and playing with field mice.

Robbyn knew the time had come for Sam to explore the wilds of their back 40. The woods, wetlands, and grassy fields became her playground. Her wild instincts were pure and simple and a delight to watch. With her new independence she became more confident. Many times Robbyn and Myles were nearly home before Samantha decided to rejoin them.

July 25th
Each time the three of us walk in the back fields, Sam wanders
further and further away from me, sometimes not returning home
until long after dark. In my heart I know it's a good thing, but it
is still sad to see her pull away from us. Today a pheasant flushed
in the air. I hope Sam had something to do with that!

A wet summer brought an abundance of life to the wetlands with plenty of opportunities for Sam to sharpen her hunting skills. She learned very quickly which animals were too big or too fast.

August 27th
Sam stalked an adult Canada goose behind a wall of cattails. With her ears and tail twitching, she burst from the greenery—but all she caught were feathers. It is hard to believe she is nearly full-grown now.

Samantha returned home less and less. Although it comforted Robbyn to know Sam was adjusting to her natural world, she still worried. They always left her cage door open and a full bowl of food if she returned for a meal. A tree house was built in the far field, high in the branches of an old walnut tree. There Robbyn could watch her fox to see that she was safe.

September 25th
Samantha discovered my scent at the tree today. She yipped once, circled the tree twice, then looked straight up into my eyes. Myles heard her bark and raced to the tree. Oh, what a reunion they had! Before she left, she marked the tree with her scent. She has accepted my presence.

One particular evening, just before sunset, Robbyn watched as Samantha strutted proudly across the open field with a rooster in her mouth.

September 29th
Huh-oh. I think Samantha has finally gotten her revenge on old Igor. Through the binoculars, I'm sure I saw a satisfied twinkle in her eyes. I better lock the chickens up at night.

Then there came a time when Samantha disappeared. As the days stretched into weeks, Robbyn grew more concerned.

October 14th
It has been two weeks since I have seen Samantha. I hope
the coyotes haven't forced her from her home...or worse.

October 21st
Week three. Still no Sam. Where is she?

October 28th
Week four. My heart is heavy with sadness. I fear the worst
for Samantha and I am afraid I will never see her again.

November 5th
Hurray! I spotted my fox curled up like a furry
red ball in the fresh snow. I am so happy.
All is well.

Seeing Sam wrapped in a warm winter coat and fattened by summer and fall's bounty, Robbyn's worries eased. With a sharp eye out for an easy meal, Corvis, the crow, often spied Sam burying her food and helped himself to a tasty snack.

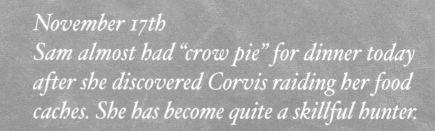

November 17th
Sam almost had "crow pie" for dinner today
after she discovered Corvis raiding her food
caches. She has become quite a skillful hunter.

Samantha's final passage back to the wild began in December. For the red fox, it is a time for the courtship dance and family beginnings. Robbyn caught fleeting glimpses of another fox marking his territory. Her patience was rewarded when she finally spied the pair together.

December 12th
This morning I followed two sets of fox tracks,
side by side, in the snow. For the last two weeks
Sam and her mate have become inseparable.

To everyone's delight, the pair began digging a den. From the tree house, Robbyn marveled at the shower of sand flying through the air as the determined foxes dug many entrances and tunnels.

March 1st
It has been a week since I have seen Samantha.
Although her devoted mate will not enter the
den, every day he leaves a portion of his catch
at the den's entrance.

Several weeks later Sam finally emerged from the den, leaner than Robbyn remembered.

March 20th
Oh what a greeting the two had! Sam sank to her belly whining
and barking and wagging her tail. The affectionate pair wrestle

Both foxes hunted tirelessly, sometimes not seeing each other for days. They took a small share for themselves but most of it was carried out of sight into the den.

April 24th
What a great morning! I was just about to leave when
Sam arrived at the den with a rabbit. She made a yipping
sound and out scrambled four fluffy brown balls of fur!
A tug of war broke out between the pups for a piece of
the rabbit, but eventually everyone got a share.

April 29th
Dusk, and the pups are still out. A nearby great
horned owl hoots. The pups should be wary of
danger fr·· ·· n above as well as on the ground

It wasn't long before the pups ventured out without their parents' coaxing.

May 15th
The pups are all out of the den, tugging at tails, nipping at ears.
They are in a constant state of play. When it seems they are finally
exhausted and have stopped for a nap, one pup pounces on another
and play begins all over again.

June 26th
Sam has become fully wild now. The short time that she spent
with us has most likely become a distant memory to her. But we
will never forget her or the joy she brought to our family. We are
proud of the small part we played in returning her to the wild.

Fox Facts

- The male fox is called a dog, the female is called a vixen, and the babies are called kits or pups.

- Red foxes are not always red. Typically their waterproof fur is rust-colored, with black legs and ears. The tip of their tail is as white as their chin and chest. They can come in a "**silver**" phase, being mostly black with silver hairs mixed in. The "**cross fox**" coloring is black with red specking, and the "**black**" coloring is black fur with no specks at all. All are variations of the red fox.

- The red fox weighs between 8 and 15 pounds.

- They are omnivorous—eating rodents, rabbits, snakes, fruits, nuts and berries, frogs, and insects.

- Foxes are one of the few species that store away surplus food for hungrier times, called food caches.

- Stalking and pouncing is their hunting technique, relying heavily on their sense of smell.

- Kits practice their hunting skills by stalking and attacking grasshoppers, butterflies, and their siblings.

- They can run 30 mph. And leap up to 15 feet.

- Life expectancy in the wild is short, usually three years, due to predators, fur trapping, and automobiles. The young are most vulnerable to coyotes, wolves, bears, and great horned owls.

- They can live as long as 16 years in captivity.

- Courtship and mating season ranges between December and March. The pair usually mate for life, reconnecting each year to start a new family.

- The pair prepare several dens, with several entrances and emergency exits.

- 3-8 kits are the average litter size. The kits nest in the den for 3-4 weeks, seeing only their mother. The male is the sole provider during the kits' first four weeks because the female never leaves the den.

- As the pups mature they join in on hunting trips to practice their hunting skills.

- The family breaks up in the fall to go their separate ways. Males leave first and travel the farthest to find new territory. Females will often stick close to home.

- Some foxes like to climb trees.

- The fox barks and yips similar to a dog and makes a mewling sound like a cat.